on first read

Ideas for developing reading skills with children from four to seven

Frances James and Ann Kerr

Illustrations by Kathie Barrs

Acknowledgements

The Authors would like to thank Daisy John, Tony Snelling, Bernice Owen and Sam McCarthy. They would also like to thank Barbara Hume and Sophie Allen for their invaluable contributions in the preparation of classroom displays.

The Publishers and Authors would also like to thank the children of East Sheen Primary School, Richmond-upon-Thames, for their contributions; and Lucy Allen and James Allen for the cover art-work.

First published in 1993 by BELAIR PUBLICATIONS LIMITED
Albert House, Apex Business Centre, Boscombe Road, Dunstable, LU5 4RL, United Kingdom

© 1993 Frances James and Anne Kerr
Reprinted 1998.
Reprinted 2004.

Children's work and displays organised by the Authors, and Barbara Hume with Sophie Allen.

Series editor: Robyn Gordon
Photography: Kelvin Freeman
Typesetting: Woodhead

Design: Direct Communications Design Ltd
Illustrations: Kathie Barrs

ISBN: 0 94788 224-3

Contents

Introduction

Reading remains the key to all learning and is a life-long source of pleasure. We all want our children to become fluent, accurate and involved readers. The aim of this book is to present a balanced range of activities to develop reading skills. We encourage all the available cueing systems - visual, phonological and contextual.

The book is divided into three sections. The first section looks at ways of drawing children's attention to the visual aspects of print and develops their understanding of the world of words. The second section introduces children to the sound system of our alphabet - how they can use their knowledge of the sounds of, and within, words for reading and writing. The third section encourages the use of context for understanding, as a cueing device and as an introduction to higher order reading skills.

These sections are by no means mutually exclusive, and children need a wide experience of all the cueing systems to build their reading competence.

Frances James and Ann Kerr

Visual Awareness of Print

ALL ABOUT BOOKS

It is important to show the children that there are many different types of reading material and books.

Make a display of a whole range of reading material. This could include catalogues, travel brochures, telephone directories, magazines, cookery books, manuals, dictionaries, comics, picture books, fiction and non fiction books etc.

It is possible to focus on different kinds of books: books without words, information books, story books etc. Talk about the different types of books and then ask the children to sort a collection of books into different categories.

Ask the children to bring their favourite book from home or school. Encourage the children to talk to the class or a group about their book and why they like it. The children may draw a picture of their book and write why they like it. Display this work or make into a book called 'Our favourite books'. Ask the children to find out from their parents what their favourite books are.

Draw the children's attention to the fact that books are written and illustrated by people. When telling a story, tell the children the name of the author and illustrator of the story. Explain what the words 'author' and 'illustrator' mean. Show the children where the names of the author and illustrator are written on the cover. Ask them if they can find the names written anywhere else in the book. When the children are reading to you, ask them to point out where the name of the author is written on their book.

Make a display of books written by one author or one illustrator. Change the display regularly.

Extend the topic to include the idea of publishing and that factories make books. Point out the different publishers and how they have different names and logos.

Visual Awareness of Print

Get the children to publish their own books. This activity may be achieved using groups of children working collaboratively. One child writes the text, one illustrates it, another types or word-processes the text and another makes the book. The children's names then appear on the finished book as author, illustrator, publisher etc. The children can incorporate a title page in their books. Talk about how some authors dedicate their books to someone special. Ask the children to whom they would wish to dedicate their book.

Show children examples of bookplates. Ask the children to design their own bookplates. Printing is a good medium for this as the children can produce a series of bookplates.

BOOK CONVENTIONS

There are certain conventions connected with books which the children have to be taught. These include the left to right sweep of print and order of the pages to be read; and the fact that one starts at the top of the page. Children also need to be able to recognise the front and back of the book.

One of the best ways of instructing children in these conventions is for the teacher to act as a model, highlighting a particular aspect to the children. Sharing 'big books' with groups of children lends itself to this approach. Use books with different formats to ensure that the children can generalise these conventions from individual examples. It is important that you check that the children have firmly understood the principles, so when sharing a book with a child ask them 'Where is the front of the book?', 'Which is the first word on the page?', 'Which is the next word?' etc.

Using two arrows, ask the children to indicate similar words.

Make a large facsimile of two pages from a book that the children know well. It is possible to ask the children to illustrate this. Make a large brightly coloured arrow. Use this with the children. Ask them to place the arrow to indicate the first word, the last word, the first page etc.

WORDS AND LETTERS

Children's first experience with words is hearing streams of speech, in which it is difficult to identify individual words. Therefore when they first come into contact with print they may not have an idea what a 'word' actually is. This will be equally true of letters.

Developing the children's concept of what words are can be done in a variety of ways.

When sharing a book with a group of children point out where the words are and as you read the text point to the individual words. If there is a limited amount of text on the page count out the number of words on a line, highlighting the spaces between the words, as these delineate the individual words. Big books are particularly useful for this activity.

Visual Awareness of Print

Having fun with long words *(see below)*

Big Breakthrough stands will reinforce the concept of words, as the words are written on individual cards. When you or the children make a sentence, emphasise the number of words in the stand.

Develop the children's sensitivity to the relationship between the sound of words and their visual appearance. The children can be asked to point out long and short words on a page. This may be developed by having words written on card. Choose two cards, one with a long word on (e.g. aeroplane) and one with a short word (e.g. dog). Say one of the words and ask the child which card she thinks that word is written on. If the child finds this difficult, repeat the word to the child, emphasising the length of the word as you say it, and simultaneously point to the length of the word.

Ask the children to think of long words that they know.
Sing the song "Supercalifragilisticexpiallydocious".

Names of monsters. Ask the children to paint pictures of monsters. They have to give their monsters very long names (see photograph above).

Teach the children that words are made of letters. The children count the numbers of letters in a word. They identify words that begin, or end, with the same letter. Playing with a typewriter or using a keyboard, will reinforce the children's concept of letters.

Concept keyboards develop children's sense of what words are. They can generate their own phrases using the keyboards with teacher designed overlays.

LEARNING WITH REBUSES

Rebus is a symbolic system, adapted by Judy van Oosterom and Kathleen Devereux from the Peabody Rebus Reading Program. It is a powerful tool for helping to develop children's appreciation of print and the associated conventions. Print is a sophisticated symbolic system and the readily accessible pictorial Rebus system can act as a 'bridge' between pictures and text for children.

A glossary of the symbols is available, as are packs of various activities. These packs encourage learning through action. It is also possible to incorporate Rebus into many classroom reading activities.

Make a bank of Rebus cards with the symbol and word written on the individual cards. Using a pre-selected set of these cards make short sentences with the children. Use a Breakthrough stand to store the children's sentences. Encourage the children to read the sentences to you and to point at the cards as they read. This will consolidate the left to right directionality of print and and the one-to-one correspondence of words. Draw the children's attention to the words as they read.

Put smaller sized Rebus cards into individual folders for children. As the children find the Rebus so easy to recognise they will quickly develop independence in making their own sentences. If following a particular topic make specialised folders.

Rebus worksheets can be used for all curriculum areas. This will decrease the children's reliance on the teacher.

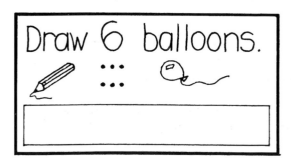

Labels around the classroom, including those illustrating displays, may be Rebused

Make Rebus versions of songs and rhymes which are used regularly in the class.

There is Rebus software available for Concept Keyboards. This will encourage the children to generate their own sentences. As the children become more aware of print the size of the Rebus can be reduced and when the children have certain words in their sight vocabulary the Rebus can be removed altogether.

Embedded Rebus are being developed. The symbol is embedded into the word and this will encourage the children to look more closely at words and the letter strings.

Visual Awareness of Print

THE ALPHABET AND LETTER NAMES

Stimuli: Alphabet books, books with illustrated letters as in medieval manuscripts, tapes of alphabet songs, any objects with a letter on, for example floor bricks.

Discussion: With the class, talk about the letters of the alphabet. Explain that the letters have names, that there are capital and lower case letters and when they are used. Find out what the children already know about the alphabet. At this stage try to ensure the children are not confused between the sounds of the letters and the names of the letters. It is much better to separate these two ideas and teach them separately. Find a large alphabet book that concentrates mainly on the letters and not words that begin with the letters. Share this with the children.

Vocabulary: Letter, name, first, second, last, middle, initial.

Activities: Print out the alphabet with both upper and lower case letters on a chart.

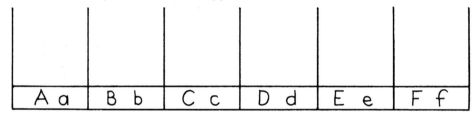

Provide the children with newspapers, magazines and handwritten material. Ask each group of children to cut out particular letters and stick them in the correct place on the chart. This helps to introduce the children to different styles of print and handwriting.

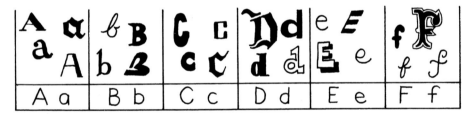

A Tile Alphabet (small group activity)

Give each child a piece of clay. Ask them to roll it out and help them form it into a square 10cmx10cm. Ask each child to make a different letter, both upper case and lower case, by 'writing' on the clay or forming the letter in clay and sticking it onto the tile. Allow to dry and then decorate and varnish the tile. Assemble the tiles for display. These can be retained for use at a later date when teaching sounds. (See photograph opposite.)

ALPHABETICAL ORDER

Stimuli:

A variety of dictionaries, card indexes, telephone books, book indexes, personal address and telephone books, encyclopaedias, school registers, illustrated alphabets (e.g. Kate Greenaway), samplers.

Starting Point:

Ask the children to look at some of the books described above. Ask them what they notice about how the books are organised. Why are they organised in this way? Why it is useful? Introduce the vocabulary 'alphabetical order'. Ask if anyone has noticed the alphabetical order being used, e.g. local or school library, calling class register, using telephone books, in offices. Ask the children if they could think of uses in the classroom e.g. personal dictionaries, storing their work, classroom books.

See A Tile Alphabet on the facing page

Activities:

• Make a class address book

Ask each child to draw themselves and write their full name, address and telephone number. Ask them to put their name and address in the correct place in the pre-prepared class address book.

• Make a word index box

This can be done either individually or with a group of children. Give each group or child a cardboard box cut in half and 26 strips of thin card. Ask them to decorate the box and write a letter on each strip. Tell them to arrange the strips alphabetically in the box and supply sheets of thin card for each section.

When children require a word for their writing they bring the correct card for the word to be written on. The cards can be given with common words already written on.

• Working in pairs, with the same dictionary, children take it in turns to choose a word. The other child must find the word as quickly as possible. They could time each other and keep a note of their own times. The aim is for each child to improve their own score. Encourage the children to think about roughly where the letters come in the alphabet, i.e. near the beginning, middle or end, and to open the dictionary in the correct place for starting the search.

• In the classroom many things can be filed alphabetically. For example, if you keep a large folder for art work this can be divided into alphabetic sections. The children can be responsible for filing their own work, and others', in the correct place.

• If the children use trays to store their work, the trays can be arranged alphabetically.

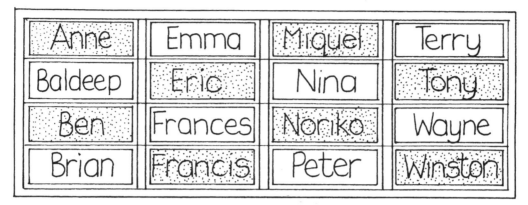

Anne	Emma	Miquel	Terry
Baldeep	Eric	Nina	Tony
Ben	Frances	Noriko	Wayne
Brian	Francis	Peter	Winston

• Cut out the 26 letters of the alphabet. Distribute them randomly to the children. Ask the children to organise themselves in a line in correct alphabetical order. When this has been successfully achieved ask the children whether they are near the beginning of the alphabet, which letter comes before and after them, etc.

• Sing the alphabet song.

DEVELOPING FAMILIARITY WITH THEIR OWN NAMES

• Label children's belongings and appropriate classroom features with their names. This will include coat pegs, drawers, their work books and reading book folders. Seek out opportunities to draw the children's attention to their names. For example when handing out books hold them up to see if the children can identify their own book. The children can make their own labels, using a range of materials.

• Draw a broad outline of the child's name. The child then decorates the letters. This can be by painting, sponge printing (using small pieces of sponge), potato printing or collage work.

Cut out a template of the child's name.

• Provide the children with a model of their name. Ask them to copy it using thin strips of play dough, or Plasticine.

• Using commercially produced letter stamps the children can print their names. Have an old typewriter available in the classroom for the children to use to write their names.

• Pictures that the children have drawn of themselves can be labelled by the children. Using old magazines the children cut out the letters of their names and then stick them on to card to make labels.

• Make a class book of all the children in the class. Use photographs or the children's drawings of themselves. Ask the children to write their names for the book.

Visual Awareness of Print

• When the children are to work in groups, place labelled lollipop or flower shapes in a pot so that the children can identify which table they are working on. The labels can also identify which child is to take the register, or deliver a message.

• Make personal individual books for the children. Use a repetitive format....Carol's house, Carol's Mum, Carol's cat etc.

• Ask the children to design nameplates for their bedrooms. Talk about how they could illustrate the nameplates with things which interest them, or that they particularly like, to make the nameplates truly personal.

• Talk about people who wear badges for their jobs (supermarket cashiers, bank tellers, policemen and women). The children then design badges for themselves or others.

• Throughout all these activities take every opportunity to draw the children's attention to the letters in their names, the names of the letters and their order.

• Prepare a bank of cards of the children's first names. It is a good idea to cover these with plastic as they will last much longer. These cards can be used for a variety of sorting activities.

- names which begin with the same letter

- names which end with the same letter

- names with the same number of letters

• When the children have sorted the cards, using the criteria you have selected, ask them to record their findings.

• Copy the names into set diagrams.

Visual Awareness of Print

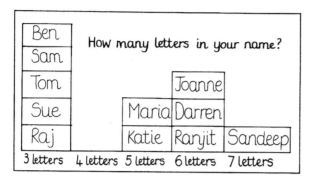

	How many letters in your name?			
Ben				
Sam				
Tom		Joanne		
Sue	Maria	Darren		
Raj	Katie	Ranjit	Sandeep	
3 letters	4 letters	5 letters	6 letters	7 letters

• Copy the names on to slips of paper and then arrange into a block graph. The block graph may be two-dimensional or stick the slips of paper on to cuboids to make a three-dimensional display.

• Suspend the cards from the ceiling as mobiles. This may be done in two ways - hang the cards from coat hangers or decorate P.E. hoops with crêpe paper and then attach the cards.

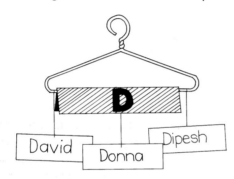

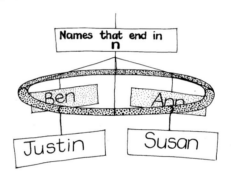

• Make smaller cards with the children's names on and then attach magnetic strips to the back of the cards. Use these cards on a magnetic board. Ask the children to match names and to carry out the sorting activities described above. Ask the children to find the longest name and the shortest name and the number of letters in these names. The children can use individual magnetic letters to copy their name using the cards as a prompt.

• When grouping children for activities use their names as criteria. This can be used in many classroom and curriculum activities. An example of this would be 'All children whose name begins with 'T' can go on the climbing frame.'

THE CHILDREN'S INITIALS

• The children's initials can be used to develop the children's knowledge of letter names.

• Talk about what initials are. Using written examples of the children's names, show them that the first letter of each name is the initial. Ensure that the children understand what a letter is. Ask the children to write, or copy, their name and to write the first letter of each name in a different colour. The children can then be asked what their initials are. The children can then see if they share the same initials with any of their peers, or with any famous person. Talk about the fact that some people have more than one name and so that they might have more than two initials. Encourage them to talk about their other names and what the initial letters of these names are. Some of these names may have a special significance, for example Kaur and Singh. Explain to the children why people have these names and why they are important to them.

• The children can make samplers of their initials. Show the children pictures of samplework and, if possible, actual examples. Talk about how people made these samplers personal by including the initials of members of their families. Ask the children to draw their initials on to a section of binka fabric and then, using different stitches, decorate the initials. These samplers can then be 'framed' and displayed. If the children are skilled at needlework they can incorporate the initials of other members of their family.

You can use this technique to make bookmarks with the children.

• Illustrated manuscript versions of the children's initials can be made. Find examples of old illustrated manuscripts. Show these to the children, drawing their attention to the different patterns and the richness of the colours. Provide the children with fine card and paints or felt-tip pens. Added impact can be achieved by using sequins or glitter to stick on to their illustrated initials.

• To heighten children's awareness of their initials, have a day or sessions during the week where you and the children refer to each other by their initials: 'A.K. and J.N. can play in the sand'. Labelling of various pieces of equipment can be done using initials, for example pencils.

• Discuss how some people have initials, called monograms, on their belongings. Talk about where you might find monograms: on towels, dressing gowns, notepaper. Show the children examples of monograms, pointing out how the initials are often intertwined. Ask the children to design their own monograms.

• 'Superman' has a type of monogram on his chest. The children can design their own 'superhero' outfit, incorporating the superhero's initial. Ask the children to find out the initials of members of staff in the school. The children then draw pictures of the staff and write their initials by the side of the picture. Children can draw pictures of their families using initials to label their pictures. Ask the children why the last initial is the same?

• Talk about famous organisations, shops etc that use initials as names - B.B.C, I.T.V., etc.

Visual Awareness of Print

PRINT IN THE CLASSROOM

An environment which is rich in print will heighten the children's awareness of the visual features of words and letters, and also reinforce the idea that print conveys meaning.

• There are many opportunities for appropriate labelling in the classroom. Ensure that there are plenty of labels, signs and notices within the classroom. These could include: named items of furniture, names of pupils on their work trays, their coat pegs, their work lists, of items stored in drawers, dinner menus, instructions on how to care for the classroom pet, calendar, weather chart, lists of topic books, fire drill notices, notices and labels associated with home corner, rules for classroom behaviour.

• Label clearly resources and equipment to which the children have access. This has the added advantage of encouraging a responsibility for the care and tidiness of the classroom.

• Make attractive notices for any class rotas. Encourage the children to read these.

• Ask the children which words they can see in the classroom. Make as long a list as possible. Discuss with the pupils the purpose of the various labels, notices, signs etc. Try to encourage the children to begin to categorise into the following headings: INSTRUCTIONS, DIRECTIONS, INFORMATION.

• Organise the children into groups of 5 or 6 children. Give each group a large piece of paper. Divide it into 3 sections. Ask the children to collect examples of instructions, directions and information signs, copy them and then display them on the large paper. This activity can be extended beyond the classroom into the school, particularly corridors, school entrance, kitchen area etc. This will help the children prepare for a visit outside the school into the neighbourhood.

• Ask the children to imagine they are visitors to the school. Ask what information they would need, what signs, labels or directions would be helpful to visitors. If the opportunity arises ask the children to interview a visitor.

• Get the children to make direction signs to the Headteacher's Office, Parents' Room, Library, Staff Room .

• If there is a forthcoming event in school ask the children to make posters and small hand-out advertising material. Discuss with the pupils the following aspects: the minimum information required; how to make an impact and catch the reader's attention; lettering styles; printing techniques, e.g. simple potato cuts for a logo; how many colours to use.

• Have as many materials and resources available as possible so children may select the appropriate medium, e.g. felt-tip pens, lettering pens, stencils, rulers, paint, ink, variety of paper and card, typewriter, word processor.

Visual Awareness of Print

• It is very helpful to establish a set of class rules with the children. These should be established with the children at the beginning of the year. Explain to the children that rules are necessary to keep people safe and to help everybody to work hard. The number of rules should be kept to a minimum. They should be simple and expressed positively. It is important to display the rules attractively and prominently in the class. Refer to the rules frequently to reinforce desired behaviour. Ask the children to illustrate the rules.

• To reinforce the rules of the class, make booklets containing the rules. The children colour these booklets and take them home to share with their parents.

x

Visual Awareness of Print

• Certain areas in the classroom will have particular rules associated with their use. An example of this is the sand tray. When a group of children uses the area ask them to tell you, or read, the appropriate rules.

• Displays of children's work provide marvellous chances for relevant and interesting labelling. The use of different medias and colours increases interest. The labels should be clearly written and, where possible, at an appropriate height so that the children can read them. The children's motivation to read the print will be increased if you are able to solicit from them what they wish to say about their work. Children should be encouraged to make appropriate notices and commentaries for displays around the classroom.

• Ensure that you talk about the displays and the associated print with the children. Ask them to point out common, or frequently recurring words. Ask them if they can find the words elsewhere in the classroom.

• When visitors, or parents, come to the classroom ask the children to show them the displays and explain the labels.

• A pet in the classroom offers the chance for notices with relevant instructions for the pet's care or information about the pet. The children generate what they wish to say about the pet and how to take care of it.

• Daily weather and date charts will develop the children's familiarity with the vocabulary associated with days etc.

WORDS IN THE ENVIRONMENT - OUTSIDE THE SCHOOL

Plan 'a walkabout' for the class in the locality. A small parade of shops would be ideal. Equip each child with a clipboard, pencil and plenty of paper. Divide the class into small groups of five or six children. Arrange to have an adult helper with each group. Ask each group to focus on particular types of signs - e.g. traffic signs, signposts, shop fronts, public buildings (libraries, Town Hall), and posters giving information about what's on. Ask the children to draw the signs they find. Encourage the helpers to talk to the children about their discoveries. If available, take a camera to photograph signs, notices etc.

Follow-up Activities:

• Draw an outline silhouette of a row of shops. Ask the children to draw the signs they found (include shop names, opening times, advertising material). Either stick directly on to the silhouette or, if the children's work is too large, display around the silhouette with string to show the correct position.

• Draw part of the road in chalk on the playground. Ask the children to make the traffic signs and direction signs and place on the road. Many games can be played with children pretending to be motorists, cyclists, pedestrians and 'lollipop men/ladies'.

• Have a copy of the Highway Code available. Ask the children to look up more signs. Talk about the significance of the different shaped signs. Cut out the triangles and circles for the children to invent their own signs. Ask the children to make signs for the classroom, the school or their bedroom .

Visual Awareness of Print

BOOK AREAS

The book corner, or reading area, is an area where print can be a focus.

It is important to make this an attractive area which will encourage the children to visit and to take advantage of a wide range of reading material. It should be a comfortable area and, if space allows, there should be different kinds of seating. A sense of privacy is often important for readers. An imaginative use of curtains can create a reading cocoon!

Books should be displayed so that it is easy to see them, which will enable the children to make an informed choice about which book they wish to look at. Displays of books (either reflecting a common theme, author, genre or type) will stimulate the childrens' interest. Label these displays to identify the particular theme. This will be increased if the children are involved in the choice of books and if the displays are changed regularly. The children's sense of ownership will be further increased if they have a responsibility for the care of the area. This may be achieved using a rota.

Any topic work being followed in the class should be supported by appropriate books, which can be incorporated into display tables and areas. Labels used in such topic work should be generated by the children. Frequently recurring words will be reinforced. Encourage the children to share the labels with others.

PLAY AREAS

If the play area is being used as a house, ensure that varied examples of reading material are available. If there is a telephone, use either a real telephone directory or get the children to make their own directory with the numbers that they feel are necessary, including friends and public services. Newspapers and magazines should be provided. (If there is a television, then a television magazine or page from a newspaper would be appropriate.) Books should be readily available for general reading, bedtime stories, cooking, etc. Provide appropriate furniture to store the books.

Converting the play area into different situations provides opportunities for introducing relevant print into the classroom.

Some ideas for print in different play areas:

Hospitals: labels on medicine bottles; notices in ward (Quiet please, Nil by mouth etc); doctors' notes; temperature charts.

Travel agents: travel brochures; posters; booking forms.

Visual Awareness of Print

The school nurse was invited in to to visit the Health Centre

Café: menus on tables or displayed on walls; waiters' order pad; bills.

Shop: price tags; special offer posters; name of shop and associated bags etc; opening times.

Bank/Office: appropriate forms; typewriter; signs in office (Manager's Office, Till Open, etc); telephone directory.

Post Office: letters, labelled pigeon holes for sorting, forms, posters.

School: books, registers.

Library: books, magazines, notices.

When a new area is established in the classroom, talk to the children about it, and highlight the print required. Involve the children in establishing the area and making many of the resources, notices etc. Structuring the children's play will focus their attention on the print.

Visual Awareness of Print

DEVELOPING A SIGHT VOCABULARY

Children learn to recognise a few words by sight quite early on and quite easily. This early facility can be enhanced and developed by teachers in the classroom. One of the most enjoyable ways is for children to write their own books.

• With a small group of children talk about books, what can be found in them, what they can be about.

• Look at a selection of books that have a fairly simple layout and storyline.

• Ask each child to say something about themselves or a favourite toy, game etc. Quickly note down the children's sentences and either type them out or print them in a blank exercise book.

• Show each child their sentence and read it back to them, pointing to each word as you read. Ask each child to 'read' their sentence. The children can then illustrate their sentences. This activity can be repeated over several sessions until they have built up their own reading book.

• The children can share their book with friends and parents.

• From each child's work select the common words that they will need to learn by sight e.g. a, and, 1, is, the, to, are, at, etc. Write these words on card or on Breakthrough to Literacy cards and place in a special box for each table, or in Breakthrough folders.

Activities for follow-up work:

• Using a magnetic board, the children can use their words to form new sentences. Give the children sentence beginnings that they need to read and then complete. e.g, I go to ....

      My name is......

      I like.............

• The words can be put on to a Concept Keyboard and the children make their sentences to form a printed book, or they can make up new sentences which can be printed and illustrated. These can be turned into books as follows:-

• Print the beginning of a sentence on the card so it can be seen each time a page is opened. The children take turns to finish the sentence, one sentence ending per page. The endings can be funny, sad, silly etc. (See photograph opposite.)

Visual Awareness of Print

• Big books can be made by the whole class or groups of children. There is the possibility for lots of repetition in these.

Give each child a piece of paper of the same size (A4 at least) and print the same beginning on each piece of paper, e.g. We like .... .Each child gives a different ending either by writing the rest of the sentence or illustrating their idea. The papers can be bound together to form a Big Book for shared readings.

• More ideas for beginnings:-

    • This is our............
    • Our school is............
    • We went to............
    • We like reading...........
    • We come to school by............

Big Books can be made of familiar stories that contain lots of repetition, e.g. The Three Bears, The Three Little Pigs etc. The children can provide the illustrations and the teacher provides the text. The sight words you want the children to learn can be highlighted when reading to them or they can be asked to find certain words they have been learning. A few pages can be selected and photocopied. Cut the sentences into individual words and ask the children to re-assemble them under the appropriate illustration.

INTRODUCING WORDS FOR A READING SCHEME

If you plan to use a particular reading scheme the following ideas will help to give the children a flying start.

• Children learn to read nouns most easily and particularly proper nouns. If the scheme you intend to use has the same setting and characters in the early books then a display can be set up in the classroom. The children can help to make models of the main characters and drawings or models of the setting. Some of the sentences from the early books in the scheme can be used as captions and the children encouraged to read them. Using the names of the main characters, the children can make up their own sentences and stories about them. These can be illustrated and displayed, or made into their own books (see photograph opposite).

• As the children begin to learn the words they can record their achievements in many ways.

For example, the words are printed on paper cut-out apples. Once you are sure the child can read each word every time they encounter it, that 'word apple' is pasted on to a tree.

Look at all the apples on my tree!

Other ideas: petals on a flower, spots on a clown's costume, bricks in a house, rings on the fingers of a hand, feathers on a bird etc.

My flower is growing!

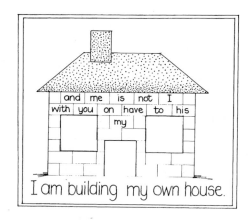

I am building my own house.

• If the scheme you intend to use does not have the same characters or setting throughout the scheme there will still be many common words the children will need to learn by sight.

Visual Awareness of Print

The following is a list of the 32 most common words in the written language. Many of the previous activities can be adapted to help children learn these words, and the games that follow can all be used for this purpose:

a	and	he	I	in	is	it	of	that	the	to
was	all	as	at	be	but	are	for	had	have	him
his	not	on	one	said	so	they	we	with	you	

Games and Activities for reinforcing a sight vocabulary

• **Snap:** print all the words you wish the children to learn at least twice on cards. The game is played in the usual way but when Snap is called the child must read that card correctly in order to win their opponent's cards.

• **Pelmanism:** This can be played with the same cards. All the cards are placed face down, in random order. Each child takes a turn to reveal two cards; if the cards match and the child can read the word, he/she keeps the cards. If they do not match or they cannot be read then they are replaced face down and the next child has his go. As the game proceeds the children begin to remember where particular cards are and they have many opportunities for reading and finding matching pairs. The child with the most cards, when all have been picked up, is the winner.

Visual Awareness of Print

Word Bingo: Make a set of cards with several of the words the children are learning on each card. No two cards should be the same. Call out the words in random order. If the word called out is on his card the child covers it with a blank piece of card. The first child to cover all his words is the winner. To check, the child reads his words back to the caller.

Crosswords: Make up simple crosswords using the words the children are learning, or ask the children to make them up for their friends to try.

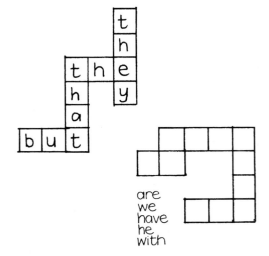

Silent Instructions: Make up short instructions using as many of the words the children have been learning as possible, and write on card. Hold them up for the children to follow. This can be used during a P.E. lesson or during a Games session in the playground.

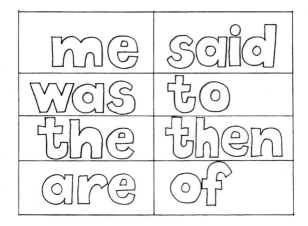

Taped Words: Write several words on a piece of card and make sufficient cards for each child to have a copy. Tape the words with instructions as follows: Colour the word "said" blue; colour the word "was" red; colour the word "then" green etc. This is a useful assessment activity.

me	said
was	to
the	then
are	of

Developing Listening Skills and Phonics Awareness

Young children may need practice in listening and attending to the sounds in words. It is important to develop good listening skills, and a vocabulary with which to talk about listening, and to encourage concentration when listening.

An easy way to start can be in the classroom, listening for sounds in the environment. Ask the children to close their eyes for several seconds and listen carefully. Ask them the following questions:

What can you hear? Which direction is the sound coming from? Who or what is making the sound?

USING TAPED SOUNDS

• Make a tape of a variety of sounds that children will be familiar with, e.g. a bell, a watch ticking, a kettle whistling, a telephone ringing, a squeaking door, a door closing, water running, rustling paper, footsteps, a vacuum cleaner, a washing machine, an electric drill, sawing wood etc. Play the tape to the children and ask them to name the object making the sound; or ask them to draw the object, or provide them with pictures of the objects so that they can hold up the correct picture.

  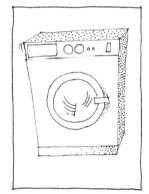

• This can be turned into a game of Listening Bingo. For a group of six children you will need to record seven different sounds. Prepare six cards with six pictures on each card - each card must be different. As the children listen to the tape they cover the appropriate picture on their card. The first child to cover all their pictures is the winner. At the end of the game the children can place all the cards face down, shuffle them well and select a new card for a new game. However, it is a good idea to change the order of the taped sounds as often as possible.

Developing Listening Skills

• Sound stories can be taped for children to listen to. They can be asked to simply tell the story to the rest of the class, or they can be asked to draw the story sequence. Initially the recording can be of familiar daily routines. For example:

> • Putting out the milk bottles for the milkman. Sound sequence: clink of bottles, water running, footsteps, door squeaking open, clink of bottles, door closing.

> • Class going to assembly. Sound sequence: lots of footsteps, chairs scraping, register being called and children answering, footsteps, children singing.

• Children can be asked to think of their own sound sequences or stories. They will need help to record them, but it helps them to think about the sounds they hear and how important the sound environment is to them.

• Some poems and nursery rhymes lend themselves to interpretation through sound. For this it is necessary to assemble a good selection of percussion instruments. These could be home made or bought, e.g. a variety of shakers, drums, cymbals, scrapers, triangles, chime bars, castanets, gongs, tambourines etc.

Can you tell the story "Funnybones" in sounds?

Record a suitable poem or rhyme, and play it several times to the children. It is a good idea to ask them to close their eyes whilst listening to encourage concentration and avoid visual stimuli. Discuss with the children how it made them feel, what pictures came into their minds and what ideas they have for the type of sounds that could go with various parts of the poem. Ask the children to build up their sound sequence - this could be taped, or they could perform it live, as the poem is read aloud. Pictures could be drawn or painted to accompany the recording. The children can set up a display of their work in part of the classroom, or it could be presented at a school assembly. Children can also make sound tapes as part of a class topic. This encourages them to listen and be more aware of the sound environment.

Examples of suitable topics: Seasons of the year - wind, rain, ice crackling, rustling leaves, bonfires crackling, thunder rumbling. Myself - familiar sounds heard at home, sounds associated with occupations of family members, themselves reading or singing or playing an instrument. Festivals and Holidays - the typical sounds associated with any festivals being studied. Animals - great scope for any animal sounds, there are many commercial tapes on the market of farm animals.

Developing Listening Skills

ACTIVITIES AND GAMES FOR LISTENING

• When giving instuctions to line up or bring work out etc. ask all the children with brown hair to come first, or all the children who walk to school, etc.

• 'Simon says' - the teacher gives various instructions but the children only obey if the instruction is prefaced with 'Simon says'.

• Whispered messages - sit the children in a circle and whisper a funny/silly message to one child, who whispers it to the next child, and so on. The last child tells the message aloud.

• Read a familiar story to the children but make some deliberate mistakes. The children must put up their hands when they hear the mistake.

• Put the chidren into pairs. Give each child an identical set of instuments (four or five is sufficient). Place the children either side of a screen so they cannot see which instrument is being played. One child selects an instrument and plays it, the other child must respond by selecting the same instrument and playing it. Initially the instruments can be quite distinct from each other, for example cymbal, triangle, drum and shaker. As the children become more able to discriminate, the instruments can be more similar in sound, for example several shakers with different materials inside, or a set of different drums. This can be developed by the first child playing a sequence of sounds or a particular rhythm that the second child copies exactly.

NURSERY RHYMES

Nursery rhymes are a very potent way of developing children's attention to the sound qualities of, and within, words.

• Take every opportunity to say nursery rhymes with the class or groups of children. When reciting rhymes, emphasise the rhyming words. To heighten the children's attention to the rhyming words, hesitate as you reach the end of a line with a rhyming word and ask the children to fill in the missing word:

Hickory, dickory, dock.
The mouse ran up the   (clock)

With frequent repetition of the nursery rhymes the children will learn them for themselves. Encourage the children to say the rhymes out loud to their friends. Hold sessions when children can repeat their favourite nursery rhymes.

• Ask the children to paint a picture of their favourite nursery rhyme. Display these pictures on the wall, or make them into a large book. Use a repetitive format for labelling the pictures. 'Karim likes Mary, Mary'. 'Keith likes Baa, Baa, Black Sheep'.

• Carry out a survey in the class of the children's favourite nursery rhymes. Cut up pieces of paper. Ask the children to draw a picture of a character from the nursery rhyme. Arrange these pieces of paper into a block graph to show the results of the survey. Extend the survey so that children ask their families, friends or members of staff in the school.

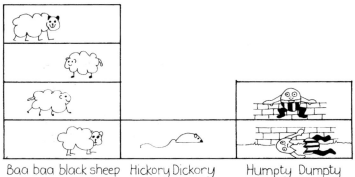

Baa baa black sheep   Hickory Dickory Dock   Humpty Dumpty

• Talk about how one can buy selections of different kinds of music, songs and poems on record, C.D. or cassette. Bring some examples to show the children. Explain to the children that they are going to make a cassette of their favourite nursery rhymes. The children take it in turns to record their particular favourite onto the cassette. Ask the children what they want to call their selection of nursery rhymes. Talk about the design of different record and cassette sleeves or covers, showing the children different examples. The children then design a cover for their cassette. Some children may wish to design a poster to advertise it. Talk about the kind of information that should be on this poster.

When the cassette is completed, make it freely available for the children to listen to when they choose. They may wish to borrow it to take it home to share with their family. Have a supply of pre-recorded nursery rhymes available for the children to listen to. Videos of animated nursery rhymes may also be shown.

Class 1B
Our Favourite Rhymes

Developing Listening Skills

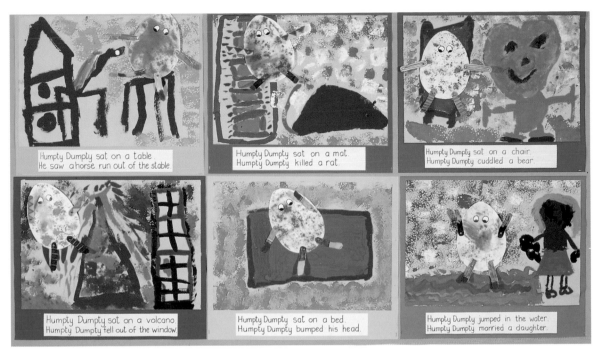

Making new versions of favourite nursery rhymes

• Many of the nursery rhymes can be used for drama sessions. Ask a group of children to say a particular nursery rhyme whilst other children enact the story. If you have a supply of suitable puppets the children can use these to create puppet versions of different nursery rhymes.

• Choose one particular nursery rhyme. Ask individual children to illustrate one line of the nursery rhyme. Write the appropriate line under each picture. If the children have painted large pictures display these, in the correct sequence, on the walls. If the children have made smaller scale pictures, collate these into individual books. Build up a collection of these books.

Miss Polly had a dolly
Who was sick, sick, sick.

She called for the doctor
To come quick, quick, quick.

• There are different versions of many well-known nursery rhymes. Incorporate these into oral sessions which you have with the children. Develop this by deliberately changing particularly well-known rhymes and asking the children to complete the rhyming couplet. This should be done orally. When the children feel confident with this technique choose one particular rhyme and, with the children, develop as many different versions as you can. Using different media (paint, collage etc.) ask the children to illustrate their new versions (see photograph above).

Developing Listening Skills

Certain nursery rhymes lend themselves to making dramatic and interesting displays.

Mary, Mary, quite contrary.

Use different materials to make Mary. The flowers are made using tissue paper and straws for the stems. The children cut out the bells from silver paper, fold the bells in half and cut out small geometric shapes.

To make the 'pretty maids', fold strips of white paper into a concertina. Draw an outline of a girl on the front of the paper, with the hands reaching the very edge of the paper. Ask the children to cut out the shape and when they unfold the paper there will be a row of girls holding hands. The children could decorate the maids.

When planning a topic for the class, seek opportunities to include nursery rhymes.

Food: Sing a Song of Sixpence
          Pease Porridge Hot
          Little Jack Horner
          Little Miss Muffett
Animals: Baa, baa, Black Sheep
          Hey, Diddle, Diddle
          Old MacDonald
          Mary had a Little Lamb
          Ride a Cock Horse
Weather: Dr Foster
          Incy Wincy Spider
          Here we go round the Mulberry Bush
Houses: There was an old woman who lived in a shoe

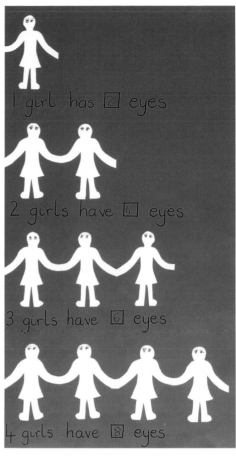

• If it is appropriate, aspects of this work can be incorporated into other curriculum areas. This display has possibilities for maths work - the silver bells and pretty maids are examples of symmetry, and the pretty maids can be used to illustrate counting in twos .

1 girl has 2 eyes

2 girls have 4 eyes

3 girls have 6 eyes

4 girls have 8 eyes

• Number rhymes not only develop children's attention to sounds but reinforce number concepts. Make friezes or class books of different number rhymes, as follows:

One, two, buckle my shoe

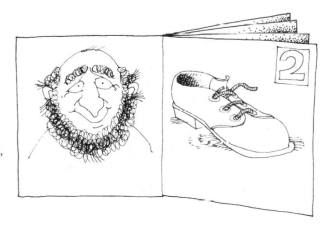

One, two, three, four, five

This old man, he played one,

Developing Listening Skills

RHYMING WORDS

As the children's knowledge of nursery rhymes increases it is important to develop the children's sensitivity to rhyming words. To truly understand this concept the children need to know certain words - sound, sounds like, word and rhymes. Endeavour to use and explain these words as you undertake the following activities.

- Make a collection of objects that rhyme and display them in the classroom

- **Simple jigsaws**

Draw two concentric circles on to card. In the centre circle draw a picture of an object from a word family. Draw other objects from the word family in the outer circle. The number of objects that you can draw will vary depending on the word family. Cut out the sections and the inner circle. Vary the size of the outer sections to give the children added clues. Shuffle a number of these circles and ask the children to remake the circles in the correct word family.

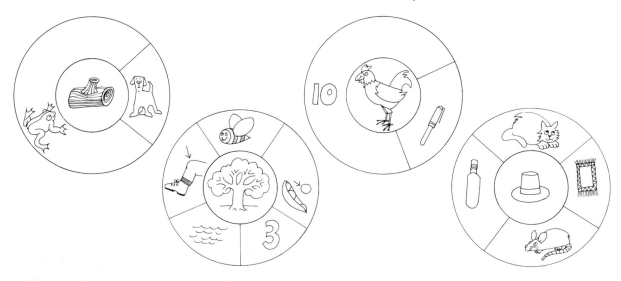

- **'Container' Rhymes**

Draw a range of different containers and cut them out. Show the containers to the children and ask them to think of words that rhyme with the container. The children then work, either individually or in groups, to draw or paint the appropriate objects which are then stuck on the containers.

Suggested containers - a sack, a box, a bag, a tin, a can, a dish, a case, a pot, a tray, a file.

If possible, make the containers from suitable material, for example use silver paper for the tin and can, cardboard for the box and the file, and hessian-type wallpaper for the sack.

A man, a pan, a fan and a van in a can   A fox and socks in a box

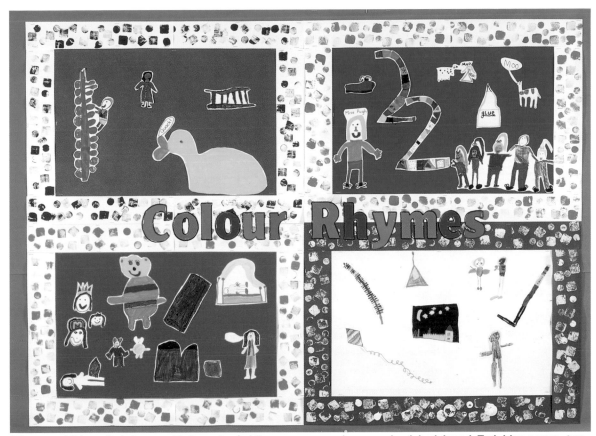

Pictures of things that rhyme with the colour of the paper, e.g. red paper - dead, bed, bread, Ted; blue paper - two, shoe, queue, glue; black paper - mac, track, quack; white paper - light, kite, night.

Colour Rhymes

Select some coloured sheets of paper - red, brown, black, blue, white and pink offer most rhyming opportunities. Divide the children into small working groups and ask them to draw objects that rhyme with their colour. The children cut out their drawings and stick them on to the coloured paper.

Family Rhymes

There are many names that rhyme, for example: Jane Wayne; Fred Ned Ted Ed; Pam Sam; Mike Spike Ike.

Discuss these names with the children. Ask the children to choose one of these 'rhyming families'. Ask them to draw or paint a picture of their chosen family. The activity can be extended by asking the children to choose a surname of the family which rhymes with the first names - Ben and Len Wren. For some families it may be possible to think of rhyming adjectives to describe the family members - Tall Paul, Vain Wayne, Dead Ned.

The children can invent stories about their families which they tell to the class or group.

Rhyming Adjectives

Choose a variety of adjectives and ask the children to think of nouns ('things') which rhyme with the describing words, e.g.

big	pig, wig, fig
small/tall	hall, ball, wall

The children illustrate the adjective/noun pairings.

Rhyming Numbers

Make a simple board game with a path from home to school. The children take it in turns to throw a dice. They may move the number of places indicated on the dice if they can think of a word that rhymes with the number. A variation of this game is to have a pile of cards with pictures on them.

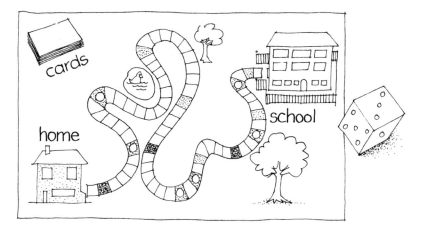

The child throws the dice, picks up a picture and has to say a word that rhymes with the object on the card before he is entitled to move his counter.

House numbers with rhyming objects

Ask the children to paint pictures of some houses. Ensure that they paint large doors. Cut round three sides of the doors, so that they will open. Display the houses in a row on the wall. The houses are numbered 1 to 10 and the numbers stuck on the outside of the doors. Ask the children for words that rhyme with the numbers. The children draw the objects. Stick the children's pictures behind the doors so that when the doors are opened you can see the rhyming objects (see photograph on facing page).

Or, cut out large numbers. The children paint or decorate the numbers and then stick on pictures of objects that rhyme with the numbers. Suspend the numbers from the ceiling or display on the wall.

weight	pine	hen
gate	vine	pen
date	wine	men
	line	

At this stage it is important to emphasise the similar sound quality of the words and it does not matter if the words are not spelt in a similar way.

Houses with doors open to reveal objects that rhyme with the house numbers (see facing page)

ALLITERATION

A sense of alliteration heightens the children's sensitivity to the initial sounds of words. Much of this work can be done orally with groups or with the whole class. When the children are fluent with such activities introduce the letters. Ensure that the children understand key words associated with alliteration - 'beginning', 'sound', 'word', 'letter'.

• Say tongue twisters with the children. Examples of tongue twisters that emphasise beginnings of words are 'Peter Piper picked a peck....' and 'She sells sea shells...'

• Play 'word tag' games.

• With a group of children start the phrase 'The fireman's cat is lazy'. A child has to repeat the phrase and add another adjective, which begins with the same letter. Continue until the children cannot remember the whole phrase or cannot think of any more adjectives. (The fireman's cat is lazy, lovely, little, loopy etc.)

• Start the phrase 'I packed my suitcase with a........bikini'. The children take it in turns to repeat the phrase and add objects which begin with the same letter.

• Extend this activity by cutting out large suit-case shapes. The children draw the objects they have 'packed' in their suitcases. Write the appropriate letter in the corner of the suitcases.

Developing Listening Skills

• Using the names of the children in the class ask them to complete the phrase '............likes............'. The preference has to begin with the same letter as the name, e.g. Martina likes marbles. Make a book of pictures that the children have drawn to illustrate the preferences.

• With the children, develop phrases or sentences about themselves. The phrases must contain as many words that begin with the same letter as the child's name as possible, e.g. 'Tiny Timothy was terribly terrified by ten terrific tigers'.

• Play 'I Spy' with the children.

• Put a variety of objects in a bag. The children put their hands into the bag and must draw out two objects that begin with the same letter. As the children are discriminating by touch, ensure that it is relatively easy to recognise the objects.

• Show the children four objects, or pictures: three of the objects begin with the same letter, one does not. Ask the children to tell you which one is the 'odd one out'. Develop this activity by asking the children to collect the objects or to draw four things and then ask their friends to identify the odd one out.

• **Matching pictures to letters.** Cut out large lower case letters. Provide the children with old magazines or catalogues. Ask them to find pictures of objects that begin with a certain letter. The children cut out the pictures and stick them on the appropriate letter (see photograph opposite).

• Make a display of alphabet books. Share the books with groups of children. Make a large class alphabet book. The children draw pictures for the book. An alternative is to make an alphabet frieze of the children's pictures.

• Either use existing examples of the children's art or ask them to paint bold pictures of a subject of their choice. Look at the painting with the child and ask them to name the things in their pictures and the letters the objects begin with. Cut out lower case letters and place them around the picture. Using drawing pins and brightly coloured strings or tape, indicate which objects begin with that letter in the painting.

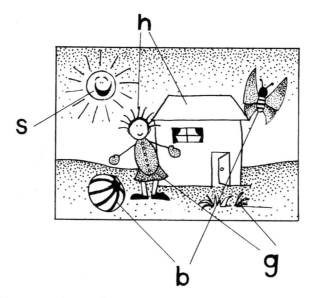

• Challenge the children to paint or draw a picture that contains as many things that begin with a given letter as possible.

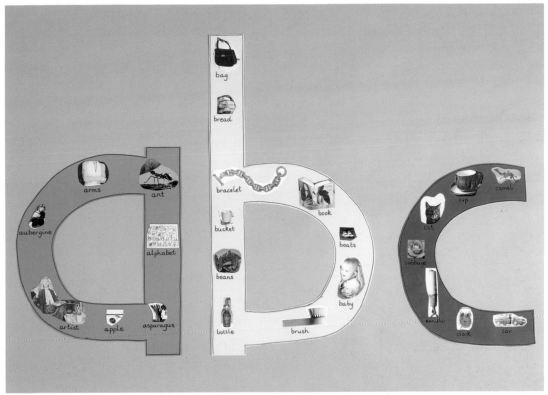

Matching pictures to letters (see facing page)

• Give a group of children some sticky labels (the small brightly coloured dot labels which you can buy are particularly appropriate for this activity). Tell them to stick one of the labels on to anything that begins with a certain letter. The children take another group of children around the class to show them where they have placed the labels.

• Make an alliterative counting book with the children, using the children's illustrations for the book.

FUN WITH CAR REGISTRATION PLATES

Take the children into the staff car park. Ask the children to write down the registration numbers and letters. When you return to the classroom, copy down one of the plates on to a large piece of paper. Explain the rationale behind the registration system. If appropriate ask the children to work out the year that certain cars were registered and whether any cars that they saw came from the local area.

Point out that sometimes the groupings of letters make words. Discover if any of the letter sequences in the registration plates that they copied made words.

Make some dummy registration plates with the two final letters which, with the addition of different initial letters, make words. Give the dummy registration plates to small groups of children and ask them to find out how many different words they can make.

F423 _AN	J759 _OT
We found:	We found:
ban pan can	cot dot got lot
fan Dan	hot not rot tot
man Nan tan	pot
van ran	

Ask the children to find out the registration numbers of their family's or friends' vehicles.

Using car registration letters, ask the children to make up silly phrases where the words begin with the letters of the registration plate.

G214 DRS	A187 WGN
David's red socks	Will George nod?
dirty real silver	Wendy goes north
dogs run slowly	Worms giggle nervously
dear Ruth slipped	William's green nose

USE OF PUPPETS TO PROMOTE ALLITERATIVE SKILLS

Make some hand or finger puppets using felt. (It may be possible to use commercially produced puppets.) The puppets should be of different animals, the names of which begin with different letters. Possible animals are a bear, cat, dog, fish, goat, horse, lion, monkey, parrot and tiger. Stitch, or stick, the initial letter of the animal on to the puppet.

Allow the children to play freely with the puppets.

Talk with the children about the animals. Draw their attention to the sound of the initial letter of the animal. Select one of the animal puppets. Ask the children to name the animal with a name that begins with the same letter, for example Robert Rabbit. Construct a story about the animal prompting the children with specific questions, the answers to which must begin with the same initial letter.

Where does Robert live?	Runcorn
What does Robert wear?	red trousers
What does Robert eat?	radishes
What does he like doing?	roller-skating
Who are his friends?	Rachel and Roland
Where does he go on holiday?	Rome
What is his favourite T.V. programme?	Red Dwarf etc.

Ask the children to illustrate the resulting description on a large piece of paper. Label the alliterative words and ask the children to see if they can notice anything about the words, trying to elicit from them that the words begin with the same letter.

Developing Listening Skills

WORD FAMILIES

Children need to be able to make the association that words that sound similar often look similar. This helps them to begin to make categories of words, and in turn helps them with both reading and spelling. Studying these word families introduces them to the letters that frequently go together in the English language and helps them to recognise and pronounce them in words which are unfamiliar.

Puppets

One introduction to word families can be through using puppets. Obtain, or make with the children, several puppets. Give each puppet a name label that can be used as part of a word family. e.g. Meg, Pat, Sid, Len, Dan etc. Make a set of cards that contain words belonging to these families:

peg, leg, beg	Ben, Jen, hen, pen, ten
cat, mat, sat, fat	can, fan, man, pan
lid, did, hid	

Place the cards all around the room. Give each child a puppet and make sure they know the name of their puppet. Tell the children that the puppets like to eat the cards for their breakfast but they can only eat the cards that rhyme with their name.

Once the children have collected all the cards for their puppet they can read them to each other and then swap puppets to play the game again.

Sorting activity

A sorting activity for word families can be by using either real objects or models of objects as follows:

Collect or make cardboard cut-outs of these objects: a pan, a cat, a dish, a train

Make a pocket on each model large enough to take a card with a word from the word family written on it. Make a set of cards with these words:

ban, can, Dan, fan, man, ran, tan	fish, dish, wish
mat, sat, fat, Pat, bat, hat, rat	rain, gain, main, pain, vain

Place the models, with their name printed on them, on a table.

Give the jumbled up word cards to the children and ask them to sort them and place them in the correct model (see photograph on facing page).

Developing Listening Skills

See Sorting Activity on facing page

Many other word families can be used in the same way.

'it' sit, fit, lit, bit, hit, kit, pit

'ot' cot, dot, got, hot, lot, not, pot, rot

'ed' bed, fed, led, Ned, red, Ted

'am' ham, jam, Pam, ram, Sam

The models can be placed around the classroom or used as part of a display for a topic, and used as word banks for when the children are engaged in their own writing. To select the words to use for this activity, the source can be either the children's reading material or their own writing.

Other Activities using Word Families:

• Children can make their own 'flipper books'. Give the children the rhyme part of a word family. Ask them to find all the real words possible and put the initial letters on pages to flip down in front of the rhyme.

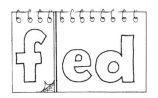

• Make labels of rhyming word pairs. Pin the labels on the children and ask them to find the person with a rhyming label. The labels can be pinned on their backs - the children then read each others to decide if they rhyme.

• **Plastic letters**

A very powerful way to introduce children to the concept of categories of words, and beginning to generate their own words, is through the use of plastic letters. For this activity you will need a good quantity of plastic letters - several of each consonant and at least six of each vowel.

Ask the children to make a word that they are already familiar with, for example, 'cat'.

Ensure they have made the word correctly. Ask the children to make another word in the same family, for example 'rat'.

Initially the children may break up the first word and start all over again. Allow them to do this but direct their attention to the sounds in the first and second word. When the children have made the second word successfully, ask them to make another word in the same family, for example, 'sat'.

• Continue in this way until the word family is exhausted. Most children will soon realise that only the initial letter needs to be changed. Working in this way, other word families can be introduced. To reinforce their learning, ask the children to write the words they have made in their personal dictionaries for use when they are writing. Class books can be made using the words children have made.

Although the first words introduced in this way should be relatively simple it is quite possible to build more complex words, for example

    Flower, tower, power
    Night, light, sight, right, might, tight
    Wing, sing, ring, king
    Clock, sock, rock, block, stock
    Gate, mate, rate, date, gate, hate

A further development would be to work with word beginnings and add different end consonants.

pen
peg
pet

pan
pin
pen

lad
led
lid

Equally it is possible to change the middle vowel and so generate new words.

44

DICE GAMES

Make a model net of a cube with sides 10 centimetres long. Remember to include the tabs for sticking the cube together.

The children draw round the model net on to white card, twice, and cut out their nets. Ask the children to think of six rhyming pairs of objects, for example tower/flower, boat/coat. They draw one of each pair on to each net. Write the name of each object under the picture. When each face of both nets has a picture, the children make the cubes, using strong glue. (If you wish the cubes to have a longer life, cover the sides with clear plastic covering.)

Small groups of children can play games with their dice. The children take turns to throw the pairs of dice. If the dice fall with a rhyming pair face upwards the child gets one point. The first child to reach a pre-decided total (for example ten points) is the winner. Encourage the children to keep their own scores. This game may be played with one set of dice, or with each child using his or her own set.

Make two dice. On one dice write an initial letter on each face. On the faces of the other dice write two letters, a vowel and a consonant, which potentially make the ending of some three letter words. Small groups of children play with the dice. Provide each child with a piece of paper and pencil. When the children throw the two dice, they place the two upright faces next to each other, with the single letter on the left hand side. They decide whether the combination of letters make a real word. If it does, they copy the word on to their paper. A pre-determined total decides the winner.

WORD FAMILY DOMINOES

This is a game for two, three or four children. Make a set of domino cards. The first half of each card has two letters which make the end of a three letter word, the second half an initial letter. Make twelve of the cards to read horizontally and twelve vertically. Write both sections towards the edge of the cards so that when two cards are placed together there will not be a large space between the first and second letters of the constructed word. Cover the cards with plastic to strengthen and protect them.

To play the game, a child deals out the cards to the players. (It may be helpful to use Breakthrough stands for the children to hold their cards.) The child on the left of the dealer begins the game by placing a card of his/her choice on the table. The next child places a card beside the first domino so that a word is made. If a child cannot make a word he misses a turn. The game continues until one child has used all his/her cards, or no one can go. The winner is the child with the fewest number of dominoes remaining. The game can be played several times, with the children recording their scores.

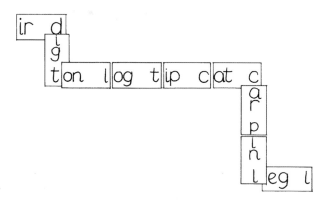

If a child has particular difficulties with such an activity, the game can be played by reducing the number of dominoes and with an adult helping to guide the child in their word building.

Suggested pairings for the dominoes:

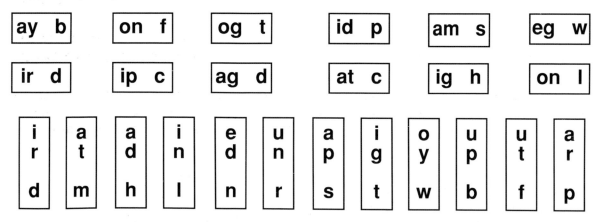

Word jigsaws (see below)

SYLLABLES

As children's ability to word build and blend sounds together increases, it can be further developed by the introduction of syllables. Initially this can be done as a listening task to identify the number of syllables in a word.

• Using the children's own names, ask them to clap the number of syllables they can hear when their name or their friends' names are spoken aloud. Percussion instruments can also be used. Children will enjoy using a puppet, with a squeaker incorporated in to it, to squeak the number of syllables in a word.

• Make word jigsaws of multisyllabic words for the children to make and read. The children can make up their own for their friends to try. Try making words into snake shapes (see photograph above).

• Give the children a page of newsprint or a magazine. Ask them to highlight all the words with a given number of syllables. See who can collect the most words. The words can be cut out and cut into their syllables. The children can try putting different ones together to make new real, or nonsense, words.

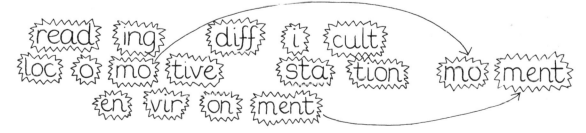

Context and Meaning

STORIES

The purpose of reading is for the reader to extract the meaning of the text. It is critical that in all activities connected with reading and its tuition that the meaning of the text or passage is emphasised. The context of the text is a powerful clue to assist readers in skilful letter recognition. The use of stories in the teaching of reading helps children to develop their sense of context and meaning.

• Telling or reading stories is an important part of the school day. Engaging the children's interest will develop their vocabulary and knowledge of the structure of language. It will encourage them to predict and to develop the 'higher-order' skills associated with reading.

• Vary the ways in which you read stories. Seek opportunities to read stories to the whole class, or to smaller groups of children, or if you have suitable volunteer or ancillary helpers, to individual children. Children can read or tell stories to each other. Elicit the help of older children from other classes to visit your class for story sessions. Invite guest story tellers into the class - the head-teacher, school nurse, community policeman or policewoman, for example.

• Change the venue for story sessions. Take the children to the school library for a story or, if the weather is pleasant, a story outside can be fun. Establish a number of areas in the classroom that are suitable for story telling. These areas should be comfortable and, if possible, have a relaxing and intimate atmosphere.

• Choose a wide range of types of story. The stories can differ in their time setting - in the past, present or future; they may have a common theme - magic, animals, princesses; they may be from different cultural backgrounds or traditions; they may be of different literary forms - traditional narrative form, rhyming stories or books without words. When telling a story to the children draw their attention to these features of the stories. If the children are choosing the story to be read, occasionally limit their choice by saying 'Choose a .... type of story'. As the children's experience of these different types widens, encourage the children to sort and classify stories. Select different types of story and ask the children to think of examples of these types. Write the different types of story on to big pieces of paper. Ask the children to draw characters from the stories and to sort them on to the appropriate sheet of paper.

This work can be extended by looking at characters in different stories. Ask the children to think of as many different words as they can to describe a particular character in a book. Record the words that the children generate.

Use different adjectives or personality traits (good, bad, evil, kind, clever). Ask the children to think of story characters that fit these descriptions. Their ideas are recorded either pictorially or with words.

Context and Meaning

• The children will have preferences for certain stories. Encourage these preferences by asking them to choose the story which you, or others, will tell. Develop the children's critical awareness by asking why they like or dislike a certain story. (It is important that they have the confidence to say that they do not like a story, but impress that it is better if they can give you a reason for their dislike.)

• Read a particular story and tell the children that they have to say one sentence about the story. Record what the children say. Write or word process the children's comments. Ask a small group of children to illustrate a part of the story and stick the class comments under the illustration.

• **Reviewing Stories - Recording**

When the children hear or read a story encourage them to review the story. Make some standard review sheets. These may ask the children to identify their favourite part of the story, the character they liked most or least, to rate the story on a ten point scale, and to identify what the story made them think of.

• Collect the children's reviews and store in a central area. When children are choosing a story, direct them to the collection of reviews suggesting that other children's views can inform their choice. Include other people's reviews of the stories: teachers, non-teaching staff, parents and others connected with the school. Show children reviews of books in newspapers and journals.

• Extend the idea of expressing an opinion to other types of books (non-fiction) and other media: television programmes, paintings, three-dimensional arts, music and dance. In all this work, endeavour to extend the children's critical vocabulary and expression.

Context and Meaning

ACTING OUT STORIES

Increasing the children's involvement and understanding of stories can be achieved in a variety of ways.

• Ask the children to act out the story. Ask small groups of children to prepare a dramatic version of a story for the whole class. A supply of dressing-up clothes will add interest for the children. Prepare a number of common animal masks which appear regularly in stories - pigs, dogs, cats and wolves. These need not be intricate. A simple head band secured firmly with an appropriate set of ears suffices. Make the masks from strong card as they will suffer considerable wear and tear.

• Allow children to enact the stories using puppets. An interesting variation on traditional puppets is to use cut-out silhouettes of the characters. Draw outlines of the main characters and features from a story on black paper. Cut out the outlines and stick on to strong card. Attach a stick to the base of the puppets. Set up a puppet theatre with a light coloured background for the children to use. If the children's drawing skills are sufficiently adept, get them to make the puppets. Careful use of lighting will enable the children to use these puppets as shadow puppets.

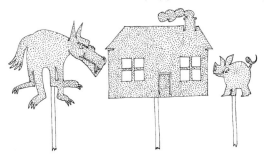

• Talk to the class about mime and how you can tell stories without using words. Explain that they have to use big gestures and movements to demonstrate how the characters feel and what is happening in the story. Use a familiar story for the children to mime.

• Taped Stories

Provide children with opportunities to listen to taped stories. When children are familiar with a story and have shown a strong liking for it, ask them to make a taped version of it for the rest of the class. This activity is appropriate for individual children or small groups of children, with children taking it in turns to tell sections of the story. The children enjoy taking these tapes home to share with their families.

• Stories and Classroom Displays

Stories provide wonderful opportunities for display in the classroom, with many children contributing to the display. Where possible, choose stories to display that link with current general topics in the class. For example if the class topic is Food, a big display of the gingerbread house from 'Hansel and Gretel' would be appropriate. Discuss with the children the types of sweets that they would find on the house. Provide a variety of materials for the children to make the sweets - for example, straws wrapped with crêpe paper for candy bars, straws and brightly coloured circles for lollipops, coloured cellophane paper for barley sugar and sweet wrappers and sugar paper shapes for jelly babies. Ask a small group of children to draw a large outline of a house. The other children arrange the sweets on the house. Paintings, drawings or collages of characters from the story are then added to the display.

• Extend this work by making sweets with the children. Peppermint creams are easy to make and do not require heating. This, too, can be used as a reading activity with the children following the instructions to make the sweets.

DEVELOPING PREDICTION SKILLS

One of the most important skills that children can develop through familiarity with stories is the ability to predict either a story line or a likely word given the preceding words.

• Most children's stories are illustrated and the children should be encouraged to recognise the utility of these pictures for providing useful clues to the story line. Tell stories from books without words, showing the children the pictures as you do so. Share such stories with individual children or small groups of children asking them to tell you the story. Send these books home for the children to share with their families. Explain to parents the purpose of this activity and what you hope to achieve from it.

• When sharing a story with children, draw their attention to the pictures before you, or they, read the text. Ask them pertinent questions about what is happening to the characters, what they can see, any changes to the characters and any potential dangers, or excitements they can identify. When children write their own stories, or you act as a scribe for their stories, ensure that they illustrate their work with a relevant picture.

• Stories with a repetitive story line are thoroughly enjoyed by children and develop early predictive skills. When telling these stories, encourage children to join in with the repetitive elements. Extend this work by providing worksheets with written cloze procedure (phrases with key words missed out - for example 'I'll huff and I'll puff and I'll.......... your house down'). For some children it may be appropriate to provide alternatives for them to fill in. Others may be able to attempt to provide the word with less support.

• Stories have a given structure. Children need to recognise the structure and particular sequence of stories. When asking a large group of children to re-tell a story, divide them into three smaller groups. Ask one group to tell the beginning of the story, one group the middle, and one the end.

• Tell a story to the children. Ask the children to re-tell the story. Assign certain sections of the story to groups, or individuals, to illustrate using whichever medium you feel appropriate. When the children have completed their illustrations, assemble the pictures and ask the children to place them in the correct story sequence. Write an appropriate caption under the pictures and display on the wall. Number the pictures to emphasise the sequence of the story.

Context and Meaning

• Encourage the children to extend their thoughts about a story by asking the question 'What would happen if............?' Ask the children to think of stories by mixing well-known characters from stories, or television programmes. Do this orally with the class as a whole, with individual children generating different ideas.

• Ask the children to sit in a circle. Get them to re-tell a story with each child taking it in turns to relate one sentence in the correct sequence. Make class books of stories with the children. Draw their attention to the numbered pages.

• Make individual concertina books for the children. Fold a rectangular piece of paper so that it opens like a concertina. Number the pages and ask the children to re-tell a story, by drawing pictures. Ask the children to generate an appropriate caption for each picture, which either you or the child writes under the picture.

• Collect some examples of cartoon stories. Show these to the children. Talk about the conventions connected with cartoons: the ways in which speech and thought are displayed, how the story line is sometimes written briefly at the top of the picture, and the sweep of the pictures. Talk about the different types of cartoons: on television, on film or in magazines or books. Choose a familiar story and get the children to draw a cartoon version of the story. When the children are confident with this technique ask them to construct their own cartoon stories.

• Many well-known stories are dramatised on television or on film. Show children videos of these stories. Talk to them about any changes they might have noted in the stories. Ask them if the characters were as they imagined them. Discuss how different stories would look on television. Describe the roles of people involved in television productions, the wardrobe department, the script editors and the director.

• Choose a story, for example Cinderella, and pretend with the children that they are a television company that is going to make a dramatic version of the story. Ask them what kind of clothes the wardrobe department would use for the different characters in different scenes. Ask a group of children to choose one character and to draw the different clothes that that character would wear at different points in the story. Talk about the script department. A group of children could decide what the characters would say in a scene. Record the children's ideas on a tape recorder and transpose them on paper, if you wish. Describe how the director uses a 'story board' to highlight the main events of the story. Commission a group of children to draw the story board. Gather together the different elements of the children's work and then enact the story with the children. If you have access to a camera, video their work. Watch the video with the children. Encourage constructive criticisms from the children to see if they feel that it can be improved in any way.

• Draw television shapes on black paper. Cut them out. Ask the children to draw pictures from different parts of the story. The children stick these pictures on to the television shapes. Display the televisions in the appropriate sequence. The pictures may be captioned or the children can add speech bubbles to indicate what the characters are saying (see photograph above).

• Discuss with the children the difference between television and radio plays. Explore how a story could be adapted to a radio play. Develop this with the children. Tape the children's dramatic version of a story.

• Develop the scope of the children's appreciation of stories by suitable questioning. When telling a story, stop at suitable stages and ask the children what a character might be thinking or how they might be feeling. Discuss a range of emotions - happy, sad, angry, jealous, frightened etc. Talk about when they feel those emotions and how you can tell what people are feeling. Ask the children to draw faces showing different emotions. The children then draw a story sequence. Under each picture they stick the face showing the emotion that the main character might be feeling at that stage of the story.

• Ask the children to paint pictures from a favourite story. Prepare thought-bubble shapes. Talk to the children about what their character might be thinking. Either transcribe what the children say to you or get the children to write the thoughts in the bubble. Stick the thought-bubble on the painting .

53

Context and Meaning

SEQUENCING

As has been described, the concept of sequencing can be developed through a detailed examination of the structure of stories. It can be further promoted by developing the children's appreciation of time, relating this closely to their own experiences at home and in school.

• The days of the week are an important sequence to establish with the children. Seek opportunities at the beginning of the day to ask the children what day it is, what day it will be tomorrow and what day it was yesterday. Write the day on the board or use a prepared date chart. Reinforce the sequence with appropriate rhymes and songs.

• School days tend to have a pattern determined by regular activities - assemblies, playtimes, dinner time, P.E., swimming. Discuss with the children when these activities occur. Talk about the kind of activities that the children are involved in at the weekends. Provide seven large pieces of paper, five of which are divided into appropriate sections to represent the school day. Divide the class into groups. Each group has the responsibility to represent pictorially the sequence of events during the day. The children who are working on the Saturday or Sunday sheets draw a selection of possible weekend activities. The completed pictures may be displayed in a number of ways. Suspend them from a washing line using pegs or secure them strongly, at the top, so that the resultant book can be flipped over on successive days. Refer to the pictures regularly to highlight the sequence to the children.

• Talk to the children about diaries and how people use them. Gather together a collection of different diaries. Through discussion, look at the different formats. Create a class diary. This may be used in two ways. If you choose to use it retrospectively, decide with the children at the end of the day what should be entered into the diary to describe what has happened during the day. (You may wish to use it to highlight individual children's good behaviour or work.) The other way of using the diary is to anticipate forthcoming events. If this is the way you opt to use the diary, check at the beginning of each day with the children if there is anything notable happening that day.

• Within the day there will be certain work tasks which you wish the children to complete. Write these on the board to allow the children to check their progress with the tasks. Some children, particularly those with learning difficulties, require more structured support for their learning. Prepare individual task lists for these children. Break down activities into small steps and, if the child is at the beginning stages of learning to read, represent the stages pictorially or with symbols (for example Rebus). These activity cards will help the children to organise their work.

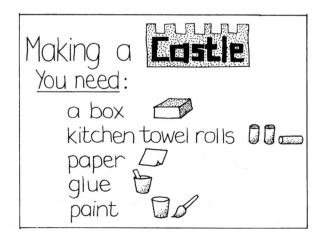

Context and Meaning

• Children's birthdays are a powerful way of introducing the months of the year. Tell the children stories that involve birthdays. Talk about when their birthdays are. Develop displays from the stories that allow you to record the children's birthdays by the months of the year. For example, cut out twelve elephants and write the name of a month on each one. The children stick a picture that they have drawn of themselves on the correct elephant. Ask the children to arrange the elephants to display in the classroom.

• Develop the concept of changes over time and the sequence of events by discussing with the children how they have changed since they were born. Ask the children to bring in photographs of themselves when they were younger. By careful questioning, draw from the children the changes that they can observe in themselves. Ask colleagues on the staff to bring in pictures of themselves when they were young. Play a game with the children to see if they can identify the members of staff in the early photographs!

• Talk with the children about how young children develop. If children have younger sisters or brothers get the children to reflect on what they can do at different stages of their development. Make individual books, or a class book, for the children. Each page will start with the phrase 'When I was ...., I could ....' Ask the children to complete the phrase - for example 'When I was one, I could walk', 'When I was two, I could talk.' etc. The children illustrate the book with appropriate pictures, or photographs, of themselves.

Context and Meaning

• When the class go on a trip or outing take a camera with you. Take photographs of different stages of the outing. When you discuss the outing with the children the photographs act as useful prompts for telling the story of the trip. Shuffle the photographs and ask groups of the children to sort them into the correct order. Stick the photographs into a book or onto a piece of paper. The children generate the accompanying captions. Encourage the children to use vocabularly associated with time - before, after, then, first, etc.

• This technique can be used for individual activities, particularly with children with sequencing difficulties. Choose an activity with a clear progression, for example making a junk model. Take photographs as the child works through the activity. When the pictures are developed, discuss with the child what they did. Get them to order the photographs and to stick them into a book.

• Extend this work by looking at examples in everyday life where print is used for instructions. Talk with the children about when people need written instructions. Collect examples of cookery books, D.I.Y. manuals, sewing patterns, construction kits, computer manuals and knitting patterns. Examine the examples with the children, compare how they are presented and look at any particular features associated with the instructions, for example the abbreviations associated with knitting patterns .

• Generate with the children a set of instructions for something that they are familiar with, such as setting up the computer, or working the cassette player. Pretend that they have to explain to a space creature how to work a piece of equipment. Ask them to write, or draw, how to do it. To test the clarity of their instructions, ask another child to follow the instructions precisely to see if the instructions are complete.

• Cookery provides an excellent opportunity for developing sequencing and reading skills. On some occasions, supply simple recipes (either written or using symbols) for the children to follow. On other occasions discuss with the children what they did and needed to make the food. Explain the meaning of the words: ingredients, equipment and method. Get the children to record their recipes, listing the ingredients and the equipment they used and the procedure they followed. (To emphasise the sequence, the different stages of the procedure can be written on separate numbered cards.) Keep these recipes for other groups of children to follow. Collate them into a class recipe book.

Context and Meaning

Sequence of the seasons

• There are examples of sequences in nature which can be usefully explored with the children. One of the most obvious is the sequence of the seasons. Talk to the children about the seasons, their names, the months that fall in each of them and the weather that you might expect to experience. Make a birthday book for the class with the children's birthdays grouped by season.

• Divide a piece of paper into four sections, one for each of the seasons. Discuss with the children the kinds of clothes that they might wear in the different seasons and the kinds of activities that they might engage in. Get the children to draw appropriate pictures of themselves in the seasons.

• Develop the work by talking to the children about the types of changes that you can notice in nature as the year progresses. Use information books to support this work. Illustrate this work by cutting out silhouettes of deciduous trees. Ask groups of children to paint appropriate leaves, depending on which season, for the trees. If you have chosen a particular tree the children can make other features - for example blossom made from tissue paper for apple trees, or acorns for oak trees. Get other groups of children to paint a seasonal background for the trees. Stick the trees on to the backgrounds and display in the correct sequence. (See photograph above of sponged pictures. The identical trunks were painted with the use of a stencil.)

• The life cycle of certain creatures has a clearly defined sequence. Ones that lend themselves to particular examination are that of the butterfly and the frog. Children will benefit from being able to observe these from first hand experience so, if at all possible, endeavour to introduce some frog spawn or butterfly eggs into the classroom. Encourage the children to observe carefully the changes that occur and to describe them accurately using appropriate vocabulary. Provide the children with hand lenses to promote accurate observation. Keep a class diary of the changes. When the creature has gone through all the stages of development, discuss with the children the major changes that they witnessed. Make a display to illustrate these stages, using arrows to emphasise the sequence of events.

There are many non-fiction and fiction books that support this work. Ensure that the children have ready access to these to develop their work.

Context and Meaning

GAMES!

Children are strongly motivated by playing games of all sorts. Games and puzzles may be used to develop a range of important reading cues and for emphasising the purpose and fun to be found in reading .

• Make some board games which require the children to follow simple written instructions. Draw a simple track on a board with a start and finish. Colour some of the squares. When a child lands on one of the coloured squares he has to pick up a matching coloured card which has a written instruction on it, for example 'Miss a turn' or 'Go on 3 squares'. When the children are familiar with such games, ask them to design their own games.

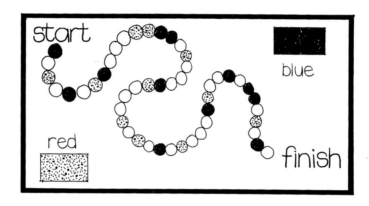

• Commercially produced games such as Happy Families will promote reading skills. If you are using a reading scheme which contains a number of families, make your own version of Happy Families to play with the children. This will reinforce the children's sight vocabulary.

• Devise simple word searches to reinforce specific vocabulary.

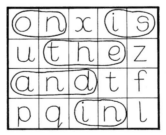

• Crosswords with pictures as clues can be used with quite young children and they enjoy playing with simple anagrams or 'letter soups'. Encourage the children to take these home to play with other members of their family.

Context and Meaning

USING INFORMATION BOOKS

Setting up a Classroom Library

This activity can support the children's wider understanding of the world of books. It can introduce them to the way libraries work and the sort of information that can be found in a library. It is to be hoped the children will become familiar with both the school library and a local library and will feel comfortable about going to a library to seek all kinds of knowledge and information.

A good starting point is to arrange a visit to a local library. Visit it first to arrange with the librarian the sort of activities you wish the children to undertake. Ask the librarian to talk to the children about her job and the service the library can offer. The children could be asked to discover where certain books are, how the books are organised (both fiction and non-fiction), what types of reference books are available, what other information is available in the library, what jobs the librarian has to do, how people borrow books, how long they can keep them etc. Back in school, make a collection of books both fiction and non-fiction. It is better to keep to four or five subjects for the non-fiction books and to select ones which are easily sorted into their categories, e.g. animals, history (or the past), cooking, dinosaurs, science, etc. About sixty books in all are necessary.

Ask groups of children to sort the books initially into fiction and non-fiction. Other children can be asked to look at the books to see if they agree with the sorting process, and discussions can follow about what constitutes a fiction and non-fiction book. Once this has been agreed, ask the children to sort the fiction books into alphabetical order and the non-fiction books into categories. Again these categories can be discussed until agreement is reached.

Context and Meaning

Set up a suitable area in the classroom that can become the class library. The following will be needed: sufficient shelving for the books, display areas, a librarian's desk, a computer (if available), boxes to use as a card index, a date stamp, a telephone, paper, pens, pencils, glue, material for covering books, coloured pencils or felt-tip pens, a note book for recording the names of library members. Ask the children to write index cards for all the books or to enter each book into a data base on the computer if one is available. Discuss with the children what information they think should be entered. The minimum would be: the author, the title and the publisher, and possibly the date of publication.

Ask the children to make their own library tickets. They should all be the same size and have the following information printed on them: name of the library, their own name and 'valid until....' The children can decorate their own cards.

The children can also design a form that has to be filled in to join their library. Ask the children what information should be recorded, for example name, address, telephone number.

Context and Meaning

Discuss with the children the rules that will be necessary for their library. This could include conduct whilst using the library, rules about borrowing books, any fines that could be imposed, care of books, numbers of books etc. The children could make posters of the rules for display in the library.

Once the library has been set up, groups of children can take it in turns to be librarians for the week. Ask each group of children to assign someone for the following tasks:

> recording books borrowed
> recording books returned
> shelving the returned books in the correct place
> setting up a display of books, posters, information
> telephone enquiries collecting fines
> book repairs
> making notices
> ordering new books
> recording new members
> finding out about community events

Ask each group to organise a library event each week. This could take the form of reading a favourite book (an adult could be asked to do the reading); talking about a favourite book; a display of drawings and paintings from a book; writing their own book to share with others; inviting a parent in to talk about their favourite book; a demonstration of how to do or make something from a book, etc.

If the class is engaged in a topic, this could be the focus of the library books for the duration of the project. In this way the library begins to be integrated into the work of the class, and can play a crucial role in supporting the children's understanding of the use and function of a library .

Our Book Week
2-6 May
Dress up as your favourite character!
★ ★ ★
Listen to a story read by our headteacher!
★ ★ ★
Come and meet a local author!
★ ★ ★
Watch an illustrator at work!
★ ★ ★
Make a book of your own!

Context and Meaning

MAKING BOOKS

Children can be actively engaged in making their own non-fiction books. This helps them begin to understand how information is gathered and recorded, the need for editing and the importance of the layout and illustrations in presenting information to others. It can begin to develop their critical faculties and their ability to generate their own facts.

There are many excellent topics for children to make books about, using information that they have discovered for themselves.

A book about a growing activity

A good starting point is a simple activity that they can write and draw about, using their own observations. An example is growing cress seeds.

The seeds are sown on some damp fabric in a saucer. The children observe and record what happens each day. Discuss with the children what they think will happen, how they will record it, what, (if any) measurements will need to be made, what vocabulary they will need for their descriptions (seeds, water, shoots, leaves, green, growth, emerging, spindly, strong, sturdy).

Once the cress has grown, and been eaten, the children can assemble the information they have gathered, and begin to plan how to present it. This is an ideal group activity. Discuss with the children which information needs to come first, second, third and so on; whether to use writing, drawings, diagrams etc.

Once the book has been completed, other groups of children can follow the instructions and compare their results. If another group has different results, say in the rate of growth of the cress, this can be a valuable discussion point as to why this should be so. It can also be helpful in encouraging children to think about the nature of factual information.

MAKING A BOOK ABOUT YOUR SCHOOL

A more wide-ranging and in-depth activity for producing a non-fiction book could be a book about the school. It is a good idea to try the more simple activities first but the people, the buildings, the lessons and the immediate environment offer tremendous scope and interest for children to discover information themselves.

Divide the class into four groups. Ask each group to be responsible for one aspect of the investigation. Give each group some headings for beginning to collect information.

PEOPLE

List all the adults connected with the school and the jobs that they do. The children can interview a selection of these people and find out the following: What are the main things they have to do? What do they enjoy about their job? What is the most difficult thing about their job?

Context and Meaning

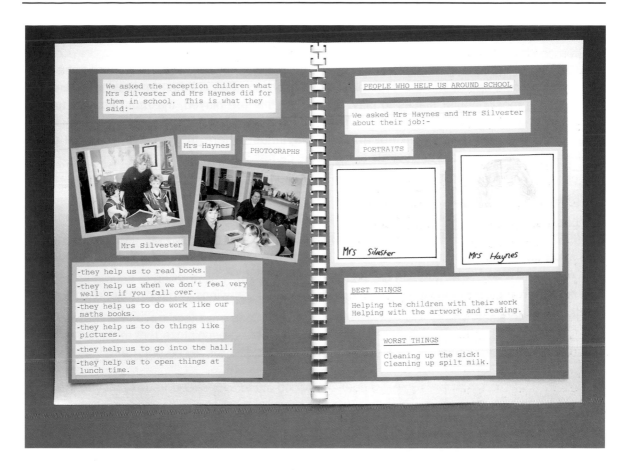

If a camera is available, the children can take photographs of the people they have interviewed, or they can draw them. It may be possible for the children to interview adults or older children who used to attend the school and ask for their memories and, in particular, how things have changed and what they enjoyed the most. The interviews can be conducted using a tape recorder, or an adult can help the children write down the information they have gathered.

BUILDINGS

Drawing a plan of a school is rather ambitious for young children but it is likely that a scale plan may exist within the school. If not, the Local Education Authority may be able to help. The children can put more detail on the plan by naming the different parts of the school and the uses of the various rooms. Ask the children to choose parts of the school to draw in detail, for example an interesting window, a brick wall (showing the type of bricklaying used), the roof (showing the material used) and so on. Short descriptions can be written about the design, the layout, the construction and the materials used. Help the children with the vocabulary they will need, for example wood, brick, concrete, glass, beams, girders, metal, iron, cement, paint, tiles, windows, doors, corridors.

LESSONS

Ask the children to list all the different types of lessons they have. Ask them to write briefly about the main things they do in the lessons. The children can visit other classrooms, especially other age groups and talk to the children about their lessons and find out any differences. They can ask for examples of work from other classes or ask those children to write about some of their lessons. A camera could be used to photograph lessons or other children's work.

REFERENCE

Learning with Rebuses: Glossary, Judy van Oosterom and Kathleen Devereux, published by EARO.

For details of further Belair publications,
please write to Libby Masters,
BELAIR PUBLICATIONS LIMITED,
Apex Business Centre,
Boscombe Road, Dunstable, LU5 4RL.

For sales and distribution in North America and South America,
INCENTIVE PUBLICATIONS,
3835 Cleghorn Avenue, Nashville, Tn 37215,
USA.

For sales and distribution in Australia,
EDUCATIONAL SUPPLIES PTY LTD,
8 Cross Street, Brookvale, NSW 2100,
Australia.

For sales and distribution (in other territories),
FOLENS PUBLISHERS,
Apex Business Centre,
Boscombe Road, Dunstable, LU5 4RL,
United Kingdom.
Email: folens@folens.com